The Imaginary Age

The Imaginary Age

Leanna Petronella

PLEIADES
P R E S S

The Pleaides Press Editors Prize Series

Warrensburg, MO

Library of Congress Control Number:
ISBN 978-0-8071-7152-3

Published by Pleiades Press

Department of English
University of Central Missouri
Warrensburg, Missouri 64093

Distributed by Louisiana State University Press

Cover Image: Annie Montgomerie, "Bonny Bove on Her 8th Birthday,"
Textiles and mixed media, 2018.
Author photo by Kelly Zhu
Book design by Sarah Nguyen
Interior design by David Wojciechowski

First Pleiades Printing, 2019

Financial support for this project has been provided by the University of
Central Missouri, the Missouri Arts Council, and the Missouri Humanities
Council, state agencies.

for Mami, Papi, and Georgina

Table of Contents

III.

Acknowledgments

I.

The Crocodile

Steer your lily pad to the crocodile. Rub her knobby ears.
Stroke her long savage nose, that old swamp dolphin.

This is the listless mud
of another bad idea. This is another toad trapped in thorn cradle,
rocking madly through the midnight.

Just follow the crocodile. She is so grass cheeked
and snake lovely. She doesn't even have a voice, but oh, how she pricks herself
up and down her jaws, as if her own private question marks
were rows and rows of teeth.

The crocodile knows how she sounds.
But she doesn't see how the fireflies have dimmed, until all of them are gone.
She thinks that an owl is tree bark clawing into bird, and underneath her
  cloak of scabs,
she is tender, white, and green.

The crocodile bursts into juice. A fisherman floats by and throws down a line.
He catches brain after brain and strings them loosely together, rebuilding the
  crocodile.

When the crocodile's blood clots, it looks like spinach.
When small bright lizards dot the bank, she is a swollen angry dream.
She's changed into her lime dress for you.
She's swaying in the mirror, with her camouflage butter thighs.

Will you place your arms around her or touch her muscle wrapped in fat?
She is a mottled shoulder, pushing through the weeds.

The Hummingbird

Blasphemous Pinocchio scrap.
Liar, growing your long nose out like a needle.

•

After hospice left,
my mother successfully killed,
we threw most of their things away.

Morphine down the toilet.
Wheelchair flung on our lawn.

We kept the IV machine, though.
We turned it into a hummingbird feeder.
The silver pole and bag swayed in our yard.

•

To make a hummingbird,
explode several peacocks.
Bottle whichever shimmering droplet
flees the feathers and pieces of beak.

•

One of my mother's friends
saw a hummingbird hovering by the funeral home.
She said, "Look, girls, there's your mother."

My mother is not a hummingbird.
Her dead body is in a vase.

•

To destroy a hummingbird,
jam nail scissors hard into the back of its head.
They will come out of its face, a death-beak.

•

My mother loved hummingbirds,
if I am going to speak the truth.

Watch, I will hold one in my hands and squeeze it
so I can carefully draw her blood with its beak.

•

And my stinger comes out of my mouth.

•

And I wear one as a necklace now, Frida Kahlo knows.
Shiny green brain of the albatross.

•

And I am a grown woman now, yet here I sit,
in my pink dress and red high heels,
zooming foil birds through the air,
humming to myself.

•

My mother died for hours.
We watched quietly.
It was raining.

We opened every door
to let the birds in.
They settled on my mother's arms.
They were oily blue and green like paint.

A palette with its low empty eggshells misses them terribly.

One Year Later

This is a mountain made of hands.

My hands, my father's hands, my sister's hands.

We keep placing one on top of another and we are building something

that loses its base and is simply grief

rising into time.

The Butterfly

A worm
with fruit peel wings
crashes to the ground.
Flabbily

he gasps
and rests beneath
his stinking orange peel
staring up at the sky.

A fly
crawls in margarine
and dots the yellow swirls
with curling black hairs.

He screams in the mirror
and shakes his damp fur:
For I am the butterfly
also.

As for me
I never said
I had rainbows
for elbows.

Never said
I'd slice thinly
for anyone
to see.

I'm veins and wind
shivering. I float.
My mind is elsewhere,
always elsewhere,

a little hand
waving from the sky.

The Tampon

I push a white finger bone
up into my body.
It is the pointer finger,
chalk stalk from corpse's knuckle.

Dance, nine-fingered skeleton.
Rattle for your missing one,
your gleaming chicken bone
creeping by the bushes,
resting in the road dust,

a lean ground-hunter
who can smell a woman's eggs,
who is crawling in the dark,
who will find her secret nest.

This is bone versus blood.
This is death reaching up
to squelch life just dripping down,
to squelch the red of not-this-time,
but I could. I really could.

We also call it stick of moonlight
or shooting up with pearls.
We have many names and stories.
Would you like to know my own?

I'd poked myself for years
but never gotten in.
Denied, my right of passage!
A ship shying from the channel.
I went back to stuffing pants with birds,
fastening their wings.

One day I tried again.
That plastic tube,

(the color of white nail polish
I had when I was twelve,

a strange time in the nineties
when I first bled
and toes wore only shimmers),
that tube slid up, at last!

I paused, my fingers at the entrance.
The instructions told me clearly,
I had to shoot the gun.
I had to loose the fluffy bullet
to make the bleeding stop.

The bullet met its mark.
The bullet stopped the gore.
A virgin death, they sometimes call it,
no one's ever called it that.

Tampon,
I've heard the way you brag.
I've seen you wave your tail.

You think that you're an ancestor.
You think you're hacking out a path
for tomorrow's twit to float right up,
you swagger to your friends and crow,
"Sex, oh man, it *owes* me!"

You hulking oaf. Absorb this:
in this period piece,
you tell tall tales to no one.
You're talking to yourself,
a cylinder high on string.

But so I'd packed myself with cotton.
I'd turned into a doll
so I could grow in water.
God, your sanitary belts
left me utterly confused,

but I was still your Margaret,
all dolled up for you
even while I greened my hair
gleefully with chlorine.

I was a teenage mermaid.
I swam with leafy head.
I had found a hole inside me

and I found it just to fill it.
A key that vanishes through a lock
is a mystery. I floated.

The March Hare at Work

Monday.
I am perfumed with butter from a spray can
and I wear a square of black lace
razored from the toast.

The White Rabbit comes in late.
His angry pink eyes are like two blood drops on a pillow.

*

A heart-shaped note on my computer screen
says *Off with your head*

and let's get some ideas in there!

I have plenty of ideas.

My electronic inbox has a coffee'd clasp.
I unlock it with my whiskers,
wires to the world.

*

Tuesday is the day no one picks me up.
I hop forlornly to my hole.

*

Tea time.
Teat time.

The teapot offers her long gray nipple
but the jam is not my friend.

It crawls down my fur, streaking purple red crumply diamonds,
then throws itself into a glass jar,
screwing on the lid.

No one joins me at the table
and with a mad smile pulls out his pocket watch.

Its hands don't move.
They don't touch me.

*

I butter the works.

*

Wednesday.
Lunch break. Reading Berryman,
my tall ears caught between the sky and my skull.
Berryman, "Berryman," I have no inner resources. Where are you now?
Are you tiny blue planets, skinned pearls on tongues?
Or do you suck small red fists of my leporine eyes…
A berry grows old, in its color of poison,
Life friends is boring. You dropped ripe from a bridge,
"Henry," our buckets weren't full.

*

Thursday.
New vows after elegy.

I will punch the clock until its face spits its arms.
I will pass my hand through wisps of a grinning cat's belly.
I will carefully move the cat's sliding layers of fat.

*

Friday.
Alice and the others stuffed a dormouse into the fax machine for kicks.

*

There will be time, there will be time.
My screensaver is the image of a peach,

like a hard orange breast covered with the yellow down
of oh, radiation, all our microwaved bones,

I click and click,

as if I could fall through a small square void
into a rainbow bumpy land where talking is not talking
and love is machined through glimpses.

*

Friday. Still here.

I leave windows open while I work,
holes that would welcome a voice,
unblinking bars at the bottom of the document.

I am so much in my yearning
that I merely add one detail to the nightmare,
buttering the clock.

What I could have done.
What I've learned from all this
is not to expect rescue from a place that's not existing.

*

Saturday.
All day in my hole beneath the ground,
"rabbit as the king of ghosts," héhé,
moving my paw from web to web,
sliding along threads of, oh, ephemeral spider shit,
drifting from violet fly to violet fly, forgetting all
as I butter individual crumbs for my fat-wrapped evening
to curl and uncurl, clench and unclench, sob, stare,
stare on.

*

Sunday.
Butter day,
the worst day.

Alice with her butter hair
is not here to sneer at me
and I miss her.

I miss even the huntsmen, who always back away from me
while I mumble to myself, while I shake sugar from my ears,

while I loose from my penis a grand arc of brown tea
as the sun falls in lit plops all around me.

Promises, Promises

Let's only bless each other
Said the priest to his cross
The cross laughed
And jumped to the ground
The priest sighed
And drearily married his left foot
To his right

And we must never be honest with each other
Vowed a man to his wife
She took away her veil
And planted flowers in her moles as he stared
It is for the best, she agreed
Applying warts to his earlobes

What can we do
I asked my body
We can twist your skull
Into star metal
But besides that

I want to sing all the songs
The man said to his coffin
The coffin opened and closed
And offered a steady beat

The Rainbow

The arc of a scene.
Beginning, middle, and end.
No, the sky's shelves. The sky's shelves for birds.
No, the sky's hair. The sky's structured mane, because the rainbow combs colors.
Or because the rainbow's a curl. Because the curl's ingrown, bending back to the earth.

Well what says the rainbow?

"Blood-red tulips, where do you think they go? A light green apple, its pillow-crystal insides?
I am the rainbow; I swallow them down. I am the shape of a tombstone.
I am a heaven for dead colors."

The rainbow stands with her legs wide apart, and this, too, is the rainbow.
Or perhaps the sky's frown is the rainbow. Miserable face after tears.

Well what says the rainbow?

"I complete my circle beneath the ground and ghosts flow into roots.
They create heads on sticks—or rainbows as embryos—flowers!"

The rainbow is hell placed in stripes. No, the rainbow is heaven, seven hard strokes of a cane.

Look, the rainbow's pedestal is air! She's supported by space!
Nothing below—that's how the rainbow betrays.

That's what I told her.
I called her an outline, a trace, and a rind. A passionate edge to a big belly of nada.
Was this an error? Could I have known the rainbow's grief and her terror?

The rainbow mulled in the sky, was reflected in lakes, finally, was absent from storms.
Then she was everywhere, at the head of parades, coupling with pennies and horseshoes,
even on cereal boxes and in them.

She bathed in spilled oil, just a glimmer in filth.
Leprechauns sniggered at how she brought them to cauldrons, how she cried, ignoring their gold.

This is how
the crazy rainbow went crazy. She wanted to organize this mess, but she failed.
As human beings, we knew. The rainbow flattened our crazy to put it in bands. In the rainbow,
we broke. No, in the rainbow, we died. We were color.

June

A lake throws wasps like toys.
Little half-birds, little alien-and-gem mutts.

I live in the heat.
The sun is like a gold person.

I think tennis is two people hitting a large green pearl with guitars.

The Angel and Her Surrogate

Inside the womb
of some mortal slut,
my son opens his eyes.

Her stomach,
a cracked wooden barrel.
New home, my son, this shed,
water and beige.

A pile of intestines at your back.
Her heart mumbling blood.
The simian hands of her soul
stroking love into your skin.

Look at her. Swinging her lungs,
the breasts she keeps inside,
full of dirty air.

How can you stand it?
From a glass bowl
shining with heaven's frost
to this.

This constant exultation,
I'm alive I'm alive.

I grew you in silence.
Pressed my belly against marble walls
to prepare you for the ice tips of my wings.

I tore apart a white rose
and placed one petal over one feeling
over and over again.

I built a still room for my son,
so still.

But He told me
to put you down into the earth.
"No one can know what we have done."

So I buried you in the soil
of a woman,
she is all fertile sleep.

The Grasshopper

Tell me, are you anything like me?
Have you ever been a finger, elbows sprouting from the knuckles? No?
Perhaps you're a well-rubbed charm of dragons? No, your life is still
  unbroken,
which I forgive, or understand, but I'm the glass jar with its heart gone.
Who knows where I have crawled?

If you're looking for a rainbow, I suggest you swap out nets.
If you're looking for me, I'll join you, and rot my ripe arcs while I'm waiting.

I guess you'll find me in an instrument, blurring certain music.
I rub my hairy legs against my body until I start to thrum,
a small scraping of your somber horns, I gasp,
and then I'm done. Relaxed at last, and tendrils limp, sprawled out
from the seed—what, all humans, buzzed away?
I play myself in loneliness. I don't know how to grieve.

Or I guess you'll find me in a garbage heap,
strolling slimy runways, dressed up in peapods and shrimpheads
as I try to tear out my peppercorn eyes.

Can you feel my sad little body?
Broken, broken me. The Frankenstein of insects.
Tiptoe past as I add leaves for wings and a grass blade for a tail.
This is my green costume, this star knotting up its limbs,
a tiny life exploded until stopped in a halted dance of prickling.
So to me it happened.

Earth,
you leave me with too many loose threads.
So much grass by the grave.

I spend my life leaping ridiculously beneath boot soles,
a small grass-covered body

flying above a larger grass-covered body because there's nowhere else to go.

It's Just Money in the Bank

The slot
between a ceramic pig's shoulder blades
is a slot.

But squint at it. Let's call it a slit.
Hold this image in your mind—
a crevice, hole-black, on the back of this pig.

You have it now? Good. Let's fill this pig up.
Pour coin after coin into her belly.

Then exchange these shrunken president heads
for a handful of gumballs or for clothes washed in foam.
Park your car for an hour.

(Bladder full of gasoline,
it sits alone by the meter and mulls its bad parenting.)

This makes sense. Profiles of presidents in a pig
for your smallest gifts to yourself. An economy.

If you can see how coins turn into objects, compare that to voting.
Pull a lever to pick out a person.
Right, it's like the coins in the pig. I just love her

and I am going to make this pig a prostitute in this poem.
(I've already hinted. Did you get it?
Do I get to be that bulb clicking on,
a hot gold tulip sticking up from your brain?)

The full pig rattles to herself.
Can she move to a higher shelf?
Can she get some new neighbors, perhaps a nice china cow,
instead of hairpins, the small metal bows of earring-backs?

When she's not looking, fingers come up the wall like a spider.
They pull the plug on her.
They take everything from her uncorked crotch.

Who made these piggy banks? Money down the slit,
coins tingling down the passage, and later, again in dark,
money forcibly removed from the pig's sealed groin?

There it is! The pig's a prostitute! Did you see it? It just happened.
Look. Look, I can transform this other thing, too. A hairbrush.

A hairbrush orders and softens what the wild head grows.
Is therefore more powerful.
Is therefore like God.
Hairbrush as God. I'm so tired.

I suppose I'm like a judge wandering her courthouse late at night.
Holding her gavel, looking at her mind.

Or perhaps a cook, alone and crazy in her kitchen,
wondering why not serve three fried feathers
in a pot of milk with blue food coloring and rum?

Why not indeed. It probably tastes fine.
Still, I find it comforting.
Anything can be anything.

Is anyone going to stop me?
I sit in my vault with coins tucked under my tongue.

I wonder what I'll turn into.
I'm trying to decide what to buy.

Bedtime Stories

You are lying on the bed (no) There is a bed (good) There is a house (fine)
Perhaps there is a bed inside the house (NO) There is a city (better) There
is a person on a bed inside a house inside the city (stop it or) There was a
place (yes) There was

The two beds in the room bond
as all beds do. Every night they flick nightmare into prayers
and kick aside the weeping monsters
wrapped around their wooden legs.
Beds are not kind,
but I don't blame them.
Here's the story:
After the gods made chairs,
they began with beds. The gods fell in love with their art
and after a time became their art.
They slumped to the ground, asleep,
and the world was left to finish itself.
The sky, forced to choose
from millions of birds for her hair every morning
blamed the beds.
The land arched her back against so many small feet
and didn't know if she felt pleasure or pain.
The sea filled with salt
just to be filled with something,
and she blamed the beds
like her sisters.

Beds became a place
for bad things.
The last animal moments before death,
the death of someone that you love,
would you like to have those moments
play out against your skin?

Dream of that,
like the beds do.

The Window

Whatever you find

looking through my body,

it's yours.

Daily Bread

This forest has been cut. Its blood sprinkles into pairs, red eyes
staining bushes. Hansel and Gretel trudge. Stepmother's stale slices
are wrapped in tattered napkins. White skulls push up through the dirt
and of course they gleam like mushrooms. In other words, you siblings:
To go home, use your crumbs. Follow the trail, live. Sacrifice the bread.

Their woodcutter and stepmother, gone. The children wander, thinking.
The witch is getting ready: she's chopped down bread, now sands off
crusts, is buttering the walls; she toasts them with a cigarette, hangs up
her gumdrop lanterns. Could any house be sweeter? The witch laughs
then fills up every crack: honey, jam, saliva. Dries it all with panting.

Dropping crumbs doesn't work. So the children take to biting. Look,
the doorknob's spurting caramel. Even the birdshit's done in frosting.
Their milk teeth rip through walls. A first smile breaks into her house
and the witch is cackling. She will kill these children with her crumbs,
she will change their sucking bodies into burning presents for herself.

The way I read this story: a woman haunts the first home. She is insanity,
she wants him, her calm man who abandons, who never notices her name
but thinks it feminine, soft syllables. The second home is haunted, a second
starving woman. The children, going back and forth, are always wrongly fed;
they trust women with their crumbs on hooks. These mad girls want them dead.

The Imaginary Age

Twin sister, in those days, our sleep traveled
down to the center of the earth. It cleaned our insides,
a busy light, each day a new four-foot someone.
Bold dolls endured repeated orphaning, adventures,
in the hard play of our summer afternoons.

Years later, I learned about the concept of flow,
Csikszentmihalyi's idea that the self gets lost
wonderfully in an act of creation.
I'd known it killing off wispy-haired relatives,
no twin girls here, just troll dolls in overalls
circling a bedroom in sudden liberation.

Hot soup with the slippery chicken: I'm still in it.
Are others beyond the wordless? Twenty-six,
I puppy-jump between my father and his girlfriend,
be my family, be my family, how dare you be my family!
In some other life, I'd be a mother now,
smug with the ability to love a husband.

So my mother died. I suppose that event redid me
into infant frump: the loss-of-parent-problem
only shared by parents' friends. Oh God
my mommy God oh mommy oh my God,
the mommyword a killing word,
I was like a cow for sobs.

I Wonder What Happens Next

1. Sister, you already know what I am going to say. We leave our mother's womb together.

2. Our stomachs flower brownly into diapers. Screaming from our cribs, we watch colorful bears bounce across television screens. It is right that a bear should have a rainbow on its stomach. It is right for that stomach to radiate goodwill.

3. We nap and bite. We choke on graham crackers and enjoy the strange red light of the apple juice glass.

4. Sister, I want to tell you a story where no one gets hurt. I want this story to be soothing, like the Little Golden books we used to read.

5. Do you remember those? Quick, happy stories with shining foil spines? I want you to examine my stories' spines and find only sketches of flowers and bees.

6. Part of me is always at the table with you, staring at you staring at me, our spoons moving in unison as we feed ourselves butter, milk, and salt.

7. Our troll dolls' pink hair rages like brains on fire.

8. The poet Mary Ruefle says, "I remember, I remember, more than I can tell. I remember heaven. I remember hell."

9. If I can have a heaven, I'd like to request this: you and me, Sister, curled up on your bed, reading chapter books together. This, upon consideration, is the happiest I've ever been, and if we could do that, sailing through the clouds together on this bed, lost in our books about plucky preteens, then that would be a pretty good heaven.

10. Sister, I fall in love without you. He slips letters in my locker.

11. Twenty years later, he kills himself.

12. Music of the middle-school bathroom: the rustling and ripping of pads.

13. I wear sparkly red lipstick. A boy hugs me hard at a dance and I keep thinking about it. You, Sister, what are you doing? I don't know.

14. I always know.

15. Our grandfather dies. We go to Mexico for the funeral. Our aunt sobs *pobre papi pobre papi* as we wait for his body to be cremated. I make my father promise that whenever he dies, he must visit me as a ghost. Does he remember that promise? What is my mother doing while her father burns? I don't know.

16. The boys in my grade are so hungry.

17. They love shit-pellet ground meat.

18. Sister, I fall in love without you. He is a Russian boy with whom I have nothing in common. But he is the first to breathe into my ear, so I imprint upon him, and it is duckling on duckling for a long time.

19. Still obsessed with the Russian.

20. You already know what I am going to say.

21. We leave our mother's womb together.

22. This is the earth of our mother's death.

23. If you scream long enough into the throat of a flower, the sound will travel down the flower's stem into the ground. You can speak to the dead this way. Try it, press your lips against a flower.

24. It's silly for flowers to act like trash, just scattered over the earth like careless beauty, so if you sober up a few roses with your news, don't feel guilty.

25. This is still true today.

26. Grief is always in New York City for me. My friend says, "You can walk down the street, crying, and no one will even notice," and this is incredibly comforting.

27. I don't like to go back to New York.

28. In Texas, the sun tries to boil me pure.

29. Sister, I fall in love without you. I find my giggle-cult of women, but it is strange to form love with words instead of eyes. Sister, our eyes navigate the tightrope between us.

30. Dearest, come to the Midwest with me. Let's invade this land of soft snow. Let's strap our cats to our chests because we don't have babies yet, but maybe someday we will? We speak to our cats like our mother spoke to us. My sister, where are you? Where are you?

II.

The Cockroach

Shellacked maggot,
rocking hard
in diorama's little chair,

let's call you Medusa's clitoris,

a jewel sliding from her body
as her suitors turn to stone.

The Fire Ants

I.

Hill Country where bluebonnets have their white throats slit,
Hill Country where I wear a short blue skirt,
Hill Country where the land grows small dark hills,

little pubic mounds, Texas, that dot the garishly slaughtered fields
of your dramatic blue flowers,

I sit on that fire ant hill
like I am trying to lay eggs on it.

II.

In the bathroom, when I look, the crotch of my underwear
crawls with red-brown ants. They leap and spark against

the white cotton like blood in a skillet, and already I feel my blood
rushing down from my head, desperate to leave my body,

to join the pop and sizzle of that seared soft crotch.

I am found and draped upon a table.
The queen with her exquisitely bitten vulva, thirty hard bites,
like the ground had something to prove.

I get it, ground. I'll bleed clear.
I'll scratch out the pus you inserted slowly,

and oh how I moaned when you pinched me with your jaws.

III.

The queen ant flutters her tiny legs.
They are like eyelashes, she knows,

and sometimes she is a red eye blinking deep inside the earth.

IV.

The bites cover me for days.
I wander in my bed, unable to sleep,

it is as if my thighs carry thirty heads
half escaping from my skin.

Look at them. The clear skulls push up
like a pimpled spill of crystal balls

and how long

until the queen's mound dries,
and collapses through its center,
and becomes a hole into the ground?

Texas,
I won't apologize.

The land strained towards my body in its own woman's shape,

and in its own raw mountains again
again my body liked it.

Alma Ashley Pettigrew

I would like to stride the wooden hallways now.
A spider has shat enough lace in the pot, I can make a new gown.
Periodically I empty the vacuum's udder and pour dust on the wedding cake
and make long sickly smiles at my visitors and offer them pieces.

They tell the housekeeper to hide the cake while I'm not looking
but she is in my cahoots and also my bloomers and instead
she finds old calendars for me and we cackle as we put the house back
twenty years for my visitors and sometimes they call the doctor.

I sleep with all the windows and that's how I get inside them.
A good glass fuck and there I am, framed, tilting with juices,
waving a handkerchief as my visitors drive off. Let them think of me tonight
with my silver bonnet and white rouge, playing leapfrog with the maid.

Who says I am unhappy? I can eat what I can catch
and these old legs jump high and far. Sometimes I feign sleep.
You try the cake and pick its lint, you freeze when I mutter in my nap,
and sometimes I stroke the spider, always straining in my lap.

Skype Date

On my back   legs in the air

         and where was I   I flowered there

against the screen   my body out

         my body pushed   its flower out

Then I was on my hands and knees for you,

ass towards the web-cam, moaning, shaking,

while a reproachful eye blinked

from between my swaying cheeks

                                   funny Cyclops

Have a flower

Have an ogre

                  Yeah baby

                  I'll flip over

Like Love

You put your fingers in me like I was a vending machine.
Like you could pull down a bag of chips if you kept rooting around
in the old corn powder and the spiders growing sick on sweet reds.

I shook like I was trying to help you. Like I was full of trash.
Your quarters were like the silver excrement of cash
that you doled out in restaurants on girls not like me.

I guess it's like this—my heart falls like a gumball
and my body's too clear. Your mouth opens below me
to catch up my heart, to chew it up slowly.

I swell pink from your lips, I shuddering break—
is this like love like love I like to make?

To an Old Virgin

You, old virgin, who is there to help you?
Your witches have retired, their potions have soured,
they drool blue-haired beneath their conical black.
Frogs doze in their laps, old greenlegs, old greenlegs,

the frogs eat frozen flies. The witches rock them for hours.
Oh, no one remembers their spells anymore.
Old virgin, you'll have to do this on your own.

You, old virgin, who is left to help you?
Your circle of nymphs has wandered off to the city.
Remember those years? You got each other through each body part
touched, but where are your girls now? They left one by one,

dragging their hymens behind them.
Now they call you as they briefcase and treadmill.
Old virgin, they did it on their own.

Woman, it's fine. You've been through so much, You've been
through the funnel of your twenties. From that whirlpool of feeling,
you dripped out a mind. You can do this on your own.

So, virgin, begin. Use what you know. Kiss, touch,
let his penis turn to stone in your hands. But it's not playing dead.
There's such life in this thing! Is this where a god
puts his insects? Yes, clear bees, eggs, and honey

tumble down from our groins, like we're machines
dropping candy, as if we've gulped coins—are we earning
or paying?—and clouds unravel from our bodies,
full of broken-off flutters of wings—

Breathe out as he enters. This is different.
This is not like fingers or tampons. This is a wall
pushing you up into yourself, no, this is you,
you are flowing, around him.

Your man looks at you. You don't have to love him,
but you can. I didn't love mine. He was gentle. It was fine.
Old virgin, sometimes I wonder why I did this on my own.

Even Now and Ever Since

Rotmanov, your name was shame for years.

I, the hideous duckling, scrambled after you
to memorize your size, your big soft body,
my fat and baby man. We were eighteen

and my heart stuck its two red halves together,
a wild silent quack, sealing itself
for a first and final time. My roommates:

a little skinny girl with her mother
and her butler, running white-gloved fingers
over beds and dressers while I stared. A sturdy blonde

who fought well, a hitting crying sister,
and who was I, the third one? Pick me up, I'd clatter,
a Russian nesting doll, a girl jumping from your hands

to find her final core of air. Rotmanov, from years ago
I see you. You stand in front of mirrors,
admiring your reflection, you stroke your leather jacket

and slick your thin hair down with water.
One night, my roommates made me wash a quilt
because they said you left your smell. I smell it still,

a friendly cheese, a sweat gone sweet
in crevices. What can I say? You pawed
and puppied me, bruised with playful hands.

We never spoke of how we touched. Even now,
the kiss between friends that crawls out
like a red bug crossing floors, the both of us quiet,

watching, that kiss gets me every time,
even if we stomp it out, our bare feet burning
with what was living in the corners of our eyes.

Rotmanov, I used you. You were a flesh poultice
with a purpose: draw out that bad soul sting.
All my sadnesses I gave to you. You never felt a thing.

I think I thank you for not noticing. I owe you
my fakest self. She got the real ones going,
like a painting of a landscape that makes its viewers

look outside. Rotmanov, I've searched for you ever since
all over every narcissist. My sweetest memory:
your nineteenth birthday in your dorm room

and alcohol is a criminal in lemons. It is the best thing
that this vodka tastes like tears should, the best thing
to be buried in your shoulder, and if music and drink

can match me, I am almost tripled enough
to start acting how I feel. Every now and then I vomited,
and that's my best memory of you, you Rotmanov,

how you held me in your arms between my heaves
into the toilet. Rotmanov, I made love with you that night,
I made it up completely. For years, I thought you'd saved me.

I've never loved like that again, my not-a-love, you Rotmanov.

My Girlfriends We Are Twenty-Seven

for Carolina Ebeid and Shamala Gallagher

What a staring life,

honey food in rings / honey rings with fruit discs / honey rings without planets,

trash of milk & honey in a yellow-gold-bee-box for my stomach of cows,

good morning.

I read pages

stained with broken tiger fingers from an aluminum bag

& I think of my friends!

O bride, grass blades lit with fireflies are the candles on your wedding cake!

You are iron curlicues on a headboard, breaking heads with calligraphy.

My other friend with her red peeled self, who coaxes the soul out like a
 splinter,

you are a dove in a cat's mouth / angel of a girl on her back / killed angel
 stuffed in a pillow,

& my friends for now we live in this state of Texas

& its lone star / five metal directions reigned in & collapsed in a field of
 bluebonnets

Throb for Throb

The woman snoring in the apartment below me
is a comfort. I like it: Her noisy face rises,
roosts beneath my bed. Down there is every vibrator
every boyfriend ever bought me. A graveyard,
sparkly pink, makes me laugh each time I find them.
Last night, my cat batted one to life. Resurrection day
for the glittered penis-finger. I heard it moving.
It rolled to its companions. "You sir! Can you budge?
What ho, Dilderson, are you breathing?" It buzzed briskly,
then got thoughtful. A spider pulls lace from its stomach
but that is burial, not grief. He, too, could pull—plastic?
some golden wires? He knew nothing of his body—
he could pull out his insides to drape his friends
and it would never be enough. He'd survived.
His buzzing slowed. I hope he found my neighbor's lips,
lost himself in her rumbling. I hope I'm not their god.
All I can do is tense and flinch, at pain or even blankness.
If they rise into my arms, I can try to tell their lives.
Maybe that will be enough, to match them throb for throb.

On Dating a Therapist

I dream of you in the pumpkin chariot.

Orange thighs swell
from the twisted gray neck of the stem
to the puckered gray dent of the asshole.

This is the sweet world of your Cinderella,
but you are racing to get home.
You miss the dirty house. All its secrets.

Bluebirds sing panicked human words.
The stepsisters watch us in the bedroom,

piggy eyes haunting from the closets,
and you talk to them over my writhing crotch
until their self-esteem improves.

Oh, my almost father. Almost doctor to so many.
You pat each mousy back and turn animals

to men, but until midnight they are wild
rats dragging unsepulchered girlish legs.

Lover, I type this poem in front of you.
You type your own work, case studies, something.
You don't see me watching you,

and I am a total pumpkin, the sun's eyeball,
so hard, and little, and angry.

I got my gold scooped out.
Guess you're richer, guess I'm poorer,

I'll get the story right.

August

A thorn enters a pink jellybean like a tack.
It makes a cat toe, twenty. My toes make feet

to walk sun-spanked concrete. Ice cream here,
vanilla scoops, amputated biceps of a butter god.

Stranger, looking everywhere but the river's
metal eyes, the fish don't see you, either.

Love Letter

You shove into me, and this is the part of you I like.
I like your cock. I use you for it. This is the worst thing
I could do to a *victim* such as you. However, you don't notice.

Your tongue tip is as soft as the end of an intestine,
my earlobe is a drop of bait, waiting to be bitten.
Hook yourself, my lover. You pound away and moan,

If I repress anything, I'll die. Later, I dream you say this
with your hands around my neck. For now, I roll my eyes
as your eyes are rolling back. Finally, you come.

I don't and need a lesson. *See how cold you are*, you say.
See how you won't let go and trust me. Oh, give it to me harder,
I can take it deeper, I can ram your cock inside

my automatic bleeder. Lover, you keep trying,
but I *never* come from you. Later, we think I'm pregnant.
You joke that you'll turn me upside down and hit me

so I squirt my sulking redness. I don't bleed for months
until we're over. Then I sit on the toilet, an open wound,
so glad to be the only vicious thing exiting my body.

Beached

I lie on a white towel.
I wear a red bikini.

Men swim in the sea.
One of my fingers crawls after them, it wants a gold stripe.
It says, hit me harder, stripe me, I want a turn.

I am hot with novels, and I am twenty-nine now.
Like a slammed rose, I flatten between pages
as someone jumps up and shakes off sand for something different.

I want something different.
I want this earth to do something new.

Earth, aren't you tired of denting the bed all by yourself?
Continents slide off you each month, leaving brown stains on the sheets.
There won't be any left soon.
Aren't you tired?

Earth, at least be my whale.
At least release me into your spume,
release me into a cloud that hovers from your head.

I'd gulp that spume,
that head-bursting heaven.

My Very Own Dinner

I cut and boil dough ringlets.
They are floured, milked, and cheesed.
My intestines receive the orange mac.

Pig of dough
unclipping your tail
and handing it to me,
the cow clots herself orange again
so I can mix the unmeat body parts and

heat it up tomorrow
heat it up tomorrow

On Marriage and Child

Bell, you keep giving birth to your clapper.
You keep pushing song through your tiny hips
like the head of my baby, the head of my baby

I won't have. Where does a mother's stomach get skin?
God has paint pots. At night he pours them over the holy mouse
revolving in its sac and growing its little heart-ball.

Is that what it's like? Is that what it's like?
I want to grow me a baby. I want my spinach to turn white
and harden into bones, I want to hear the forming feet erupt

ten heads, the perfect toes. Listen, a wand is spurting from its star.
Who loves like that? Who loves enough and away
to want a combination of me and you?

Not me and not you. I have thought around love
and it seems very strange and unlikely. I am too specific
and made of apple parts or faucet rust so I laugh

and how could any person ever love another person all
full up with traits, jangling like paperclips or acorns
or cubes of frozen unicorn urine and if I loved,

how could I ever, with me over here and you over there,
with us masturbating as we squint unbelievingly through telescopes
at whatever fills a human bag making more loved trash?

The Gummy Bear

Jewel bear, fetal bear, whirls-in-fur-stomach bear,
deep charm, bait charm, heart-casts-its-head-on-string charm,
                bone thread, a long way, headless heart on catch day,

and the rainbow played with her last teardrop
before placing it gently into the ursine uterus.

                        The mother bear wrenched herself through snow,
white sky cutting bird legs from their bodies. They fell on her like twigs. She ran.
Hair on the trees stood up and fell off. Green needles on the forest floor.
The birds could only fly now, she could only run,

                and this was her own light, strung in her own belly,
and even if she evaporated, her bones breaking into clouds,
she would stop at nothing to bury her baby into snow.

The licked embryo sank into the ground.
Left there for that long winter, it grew hair and eyes even in its sleep.

One day it floats out beautiful,
            a balloon on its umbilical,
                    wondering why, and to where, and for whom.

Infandum

I.

The smallest devil
is named *Leukemia*.

A red girl
in pigtails, black teeth, black eyes,
a smell like sugar burning.

Her pleasure is to turn blood white,
and for that she can be mistaken

for an angel.
Leukos, white, *aima*, blood.
Veins flow with milk.

Leukemia knows she's a cow.
She laughs in her playhouse of bones.

II.

What I remember
is my mother
trying to turn the milk to wine.

When you're almost dead,
why not try your hand at god?

My mother wanted red blood,

and *Leukemia*, don't you dare
make my mother's deathbed silly,

don't you dare call her *vampire*,
don't you dare bald her and swell her,
don't you dare ever to describe her—

So. My mother wanted blood.
Propped up in her hospice bed,

she ate steak after steak.
We fed her every bite,

and I was afraid she would choke.
My father said, *It doesn't matter now*,

but it did. Who wants to die choking?
Who wants to die, period? She didn't die choking

but she did die in pain, in fear,
and this is something

I can't turn into something else.

III.

When Aeneas tells Dido about the fall of Troy,

he says, *Infandum, regina,
jubes renovare dolorem.*

Queen, you order me to relive
unspeakable pain.

Infandum. Unspeakable. I was taking Latin in school
and the drama of the word appealed to me.

Around that time, my mother began
a rule called *sobremesa*.

It was mostly for my father
because after dinner, he always sprang up from the table
to whisk away dishes, to clean

while my sister and mother and I sat
hablando hablando hablando

until one day my mother shouted,
Sobremesa! Around the table!

She wanted to take her time
eating with us, talking with us,

but my father never could stand to sit still.

IV.

In the moments before my mother died,
I was looking at a picture of the four of us.

Her breaths were guttural, with almost minutes in between,
and my father said, *I've heard this sound before* (when?
I've never asked him when), *come here, tell her you love her.*

We did, over and over,
and she died.

Right away, the hospice aid began to flush the morphine.
I remember watching her flush the pills,
and I remember thinking her urgency was rude.

Then I don't remember anything

for days after that.

Years later, my father tells me

that he'd felt like he was trying to fight a fire,
calling doctors, trying to work, trying to comfort

the teeming terror of his daughters.
He got to watch our brains

burn like two blue flowers
that go permanently black

at the edges, he got to watch that,

but at least when she was sick he could *do* something.
After my mother died, there was nothing.
My father sat alone at a table. He didn't talk.

He told no one.

III.

To Go to Marco

Marco lives with his grandfather.

I only ever see the grandfather from the knees down.

Marco is three or four. Our age. He speaks Spanish.

You go through the back of Georgina's closet to get there.

Georgina is my twin sister.

Marco is her imaginary friend.

He is *her* imaginary friend.

I can see him.

*

A tree is full of green heads. It thinks so much, a green thinking that holds birds. These green thoughts are exponential and celestial, paused only by the occasional nest. What shall I make? the tree wonders. Each egg travels down the curved tube of a question mark.

Home is a braid, pinned fancy and rough. Home is a stomach, left in a tree.

*

An old man named Ernie lives next door. He has a shiny bald head. When he works in his yard, he calls to us through the fence. "Hey, girls!" he says. When we are seven, he dies from a heart attack. A few weeks or maybe months later, we hear "Hey, girls!" through the fence.

We never talk about this. Years later, Georgina turns to me and says, "Remember when we heard Ernie after he died?" "Oh, yeah," I say, and we go back to whatever we are doing.

Georgina, we step in and out of each other. We haunt each other casually.

Hi hell-face.
Hi hell-face.

This morning the sun gave birth to its spokes. Look, you can see it there
in the sky. It took so long, because you know how spokes are, all gathered
in the center. But every mother dissolves a knot in order to produce. Now
this gold wheel wears its children. Ah, if only every crown was made from
its own pushed loveliness! But already the children are trying to leave. See
how they pull in different directions.

*

Wasps buzz through our childhood. Their nests line the walk to our house.
Georgina and I run from the car to the door as our mother walks slowly
behind. We don't know that the wasps are clockwork parts, springs and
gears and hands, ticking us to adulthood.

When we are seven, there is a little girl in our class whom we hate. We call
her "Weewa" as a code name so we can discuss our hatred of her at school,
since talking about her at home isn't enough. "Look at that smelly Weewa,"
we say at recess, eying her disapprovingly as she plays she is a horse all by
herself.

We form an "I Hate Weewa" club with our friend Rachel. In Rachel's
backyard, we build a fort out of branches and lumber. It is our clubhouse.
As we crouch inside the lattice of wood scraps, it is like we are trapped
beneath an overturned nest. Bad, bad baby birds. We write lists of
everything we hate about Weewa and draw pictures of us farting on her.
Wasps crawl over our dome and contribute angry buzzes.

*

Egg with two yolks:
out of the shell,
we slide away from each other.

I guess God laid us.
I guess God made us,

62

our cloudy bodies
crisping in a pan.

Georgina,
I break and leak towards you,
but can't push through
the borders of our skin.

God's a chicken.
His head droops
with red organs.

*

I am trying to tell you what home is. I rest in my memories, in the way-backness, and it is so present. Georgina, do you remember the slide shaped like an elephant? Do you remember the red boards of the deck? My childhood was a safe, dark pocket. Now, nothing feels like my childhood did. I am always in such danger now, the danger of the nearer past, the danger of my less lyrical body.

I was a beloved child. I think we always cherish our children, but eventually, we get used to them. I want that, the incredible surge of look what we made, and then the please honey, I am trying to cook dinner, will you find something else to do.

*

When I am thirteen, I have a stuffed orange hippopotamus, about the size of a Beanie Baby, named Harry. My father decides Harry is his nemesis, and crams him into hiding places (the freezer, my desk drawer) with little notes: "Help me!" "He's coming for me!"

I rescue Harry and place him in my father's shoes, by his toothbrush. I leave notes, too: "My revenge will be slow," "I am always watching," and, sometimes, just "Hawwwwwwwwwy."

Once, I find Harry swinging from my ceiling fan, a piece of yarn tied around his throat. I laugh and laugh. Too young to find this anything but hilarious, too old to be playing this little game of death.

When we are eight or nine, Georgina and I invent a third twin, Margaret. She is the scapegoat: "Who ate the last cookie?" "Margaret did!" "Who keeps sneaking out of bed?" "Margaret does!" In photo albums, Georgina and I sometimes leave room "for Margaret." Our arms drape the waist of a blank space.

Marco, is that how we hid you? Was that you visiting, trembling between us?

*

One summer, our parents throw a party and exile us to their bedroom. Languidly, we snoop. On a shelf in the closet, we find small yellow boxes, the kind worry dolls come in. Worry dolls are the size of toothpicks, little woven dresses and pants. Tiny Scream-like faces. We open the boxes. We find our baby teeth.

If you give a worry doll to a child, she tells the doll her worries, then puts it underneath her pillow. As the child sleeps, the doll absorbs every fear.

If you put a tooth below a pillow, what do you leave behind? Strange, how bones keep pushing through our gums. Is it a birth or a death? Rows of white tombstones.

That little girl
Her smile
Full of doll-worries

*

These memories
Sloppy jewels in jars

*

Georgina and I play a computer game where you make mazes for worms to crawl through. The point of the game is probably to develop hand-eye coordination, or visual-spatial intelligence, but Georgina and I have one goal only, and that is to torture the worms past all psychological endurance.

Clicking carefully with the mouse, we draw very small squares, as small as possible, so that a worm can barely turn around in its little cell. It makes horrible clinking sounds as it bangs against the walls. We laugh maniacally. It is good practice for the Oregon Trail, which we will play in a few years and use to repeatedly kill off Weewa.

*

Sometimes
I feel like a butterfly,

a flower
with its insides pulled out.

My guts decorate
the double canvas
of my wings.

*

I can't speak Spanish anymore. Marco, did you take my Spanish with you when you left? I want it back. I want my double-tongue, my mouth pushing out two red bellies instead of one.

*

Georgina and I get Popples for Christmas. You remember Popples, those small, bearlike creatures that can be tucked into their own pouches and rolled into balls. They have soft tufts of fur on their head and festive pom-poms on their tails. Their expression is cheerfully dazed. Mine is pink; Georgina's purple.

I want to be a Popple. I want to crawl into my stomach, or maybe down my own throat. Would I be kinder to myself then? Here I go, headfirst! It is dark and I bump into my bones. I can see my own heart! I kiss it. It kisses back. Maybe we make out. Now I am rolling away from every single one of you.

*

I watch old home videos. Look, everyone is so much younger! Look, Georgina and I are beautiful! We are beautiful because we are three years old, and all three-year-olds are beautiful. I think of my step-nephews, who are small and blonde, sweet ducks whom all of us adore. Still, I prepare to say goodbye to their beauty. Even as I play with them, even as they are three and five years old forever, I say goodbye goodbye goodbye.

One day my step-nephews may be sad like me, thirty-plus years old, watching videos of their young parents, watching videos of their beautiful selves. They will watch their birthday parties and Christmases, when everyone is stressed and young and thoughtless in their beauty. I am in these videos, I am stressed and young and therefore thoughtless in my beauty, but I have my own past to memorize. I leave this to become their past, their film to excavate for clues.

*

Here I am, in memory's safe, dark pocket. Oh no, there are also wasps and teeth. Worms from the maze, I hope you found good therapists, patient middle-aged worms with tailored suits and good haircuts. Weewa, I heard you turned anorexic, went away for a while. Now you have a husband and baby. You gallop in adulthood, lean, confident, running the right race, while I keep nosing through the womb. Maybe this is justice. Relieved, I click through your pictures.

*

I know we hold hands until the end, Georgina. I know we cling, our tiny wet hands soothing each other. We look for a while, and then we let each other go, and you give yourself to the shuddering muscle of our sky. I stay awhile, numb, catastrophic in a world without you, and then I too climb into the sky.

*

Marco has olive skin and black hair.

A small white dog runs around us.

We sit at Grandfather's knees.

This is how you go to Marco's house:

Fall back into blackness.

Blink your eyes, and you are there.

Acknowledgments

Special thanks to the Michener Center for Writers at the University of Texas in Austin, especially Dean Young and Brigit Pegeen Kelly (rest in peace), whose brilliance and weird sparkle will mark me forever. Thanks also to Shamala Gallagher, Carolina Ebeid, and Kevin Powers, the other members of the fabulous four. Jim Magnuson, Marla Akin, Debbie Dewees, and Michael Adams—thank you for believing in me.

For the various ways they have shaped my thinking and writing, many thanks also are due to Peter Richards, Jorie Graham, Marie Ponsot, Mary Ruefle, Gabriel Fried, and Anand Prahlad. I thank, too, some formative childhood teachers and experiences: Beth Utley and Rita Guffey, as well as Writers in the Schools in Houston.

Thank you to everyone at Pleiades Press, especially Jenny Molberg. Thank you to Annie Montgomerie for letting me use her fretful cow to grace my cover. Thank you to Melissa Broder for her early encouragement. Thank you to Kathryn Nuernberger.

Thank you to my writing groups over the years, especially the New York group and Kate Harlin and Carli Sinclair (stir the pot!).

I thank Adrienne Fisher, for her dearness and squishiness. Other beloved friends and family, I thank you, including Jen Julian, Joanna Eleftheriou, Kavita Pillai, Corinna Cook, my *Missouri Review* crew, and Ragtag. Kisses to Chloe for all her "help."

To my father, Richard Petronella, and my sister, Georgina Petronella, I love you and I thank you.

To my mother, my mystery. Olga Flores, 1945-2005.

Thanks to the editors of the following publications in which these poems have appeared, sometimes in slightly different versions.

Beloit Poetry Journal: "One Year Later"
Birmingham Poetry Review: "Beached"
Brevity: "I Wonder What Happens Next"
Borderlands: Texas Poetry Review: "My Girlfriends We Are Twenty-Seven"
CutBank: "The March Hare at Work"
ElevenEleven: "The Fire Ants," "On Marriage and Child"
HTMLGIANT: "Promises, Promises"
La Petite Zine: "The Tampon"
Origins Journal: "The Imaginary Age," "Alma Ashley Pettigrew,"
  "To an Old Virgin"
Pleiades: "On Dating a Therapist," "The Angel and Her Surrogate"
Quarterly West: "June," "Bedtime Stories," *Infandum*
Southwest Review: "Like Love," "Throb for Throb"
Third Coast: "The Rainbow"
Transom Journal: "The Gummy Bear"
Unstuck: "The Butterfly, "The Cockroach," "The Crocodile,"
  "The Grasshopper," "The Hummingbird"

ABOUT THE AUTHOR

Leanna Petronella's poetry appears in *Beloit Poetry Journal*, *Third Coast*, *Birmingham Poetry Review*, *CutBank*, *Quarterly West*, and other publications. Her fiction appears in *Drunken Boat*, and her nonfiction appears in *Brevity*. She holds a PhD from the University of Missouri and an MFA from the Michener Center for Writers at the University of Texas. She lives in Austin, Texas.

THE EDITORS PRIZE FOR POETRY

The editors at Pleaides Press select 10-15 finalists from among those manuscripts submitted each year. The director, along with a panel of members of the Pleaides Press Advisory Board, selects one winner for publication. All selections are made blind to authorship in a contest in an open competition for which any poet writing in English is eligible. Pleiades Press Editors Prize for Poetry books are distributed by Louisiana State University Press.

ALSO AVAILABLE FROM PLEIADES PRESS

dark // thing by Ashley M. Jones

Destruction of the Lover by Luis Panini, translated by Lawrence Schimel

Fluid States by Heidi Czerwiec

30 Questions People Don't Ask by Inga Gaile, translated by Ieva Lesinka

The Poem's Country: Place & Poetic Practice, edited by Shara Lessley & Bruce Snider

In Between: Poetry Comics by Mita Mahato

Country House by Sarah Barber

How to Tell If You Are Human, Diagram Poems by Jessy Randall

Bridled by Amy Meng

The Darkness Call by Gary Fincke

A Lesser Love by E.J. Koh

Novena by Jacques J. Rancourt

Book of No Ledge: Visual Poems by Nance Van Winckel

Landscape with Headless Mama by Jennifer Ghivan

Random Exorcisms by Adrian C. Louis

Poetry Comics from the Book of Hours by Bianca Stone

The Belle Mar by Katie Bickham